The World's Best Women Jokes

John Thomas

ILLUSTRATED BY
FRANK DICKENS

HarperCollins*Publishers*

HarperCollins*Publishers*
77–85 Fulham Palace Road,
Hammersmith, London W6 8JB

A Paperback Original 1996
3 5 7 9 8 6 4

A catalogue record for this book
is available from the British Library

ISBN 0 00 638823 X

Photoset in Linotron Goudy Old Style by
Rowland Phototypesetting Limited
Bury St Edmunds, Suffolk

Printed in Great Britain by
Clays Lts, St Ives plc

There are two ways to handle women.
Both are wrong.

How do you make a hormone?
Put sand in the Vaseline.

A woman called a newspaper after the death of her husband to ask how much a death notice costs. Five pounds a word, she was told.

'OK,' she said, 'put "Mort is dead".'

'Is that all?' the newspaper man asked. 'It's actually five pounds per word only after the first sentence.'

'Oh,' said the woman, 'in that case, put "Mort is dead. Volvo for sale."'

First girl: I have an awful complaint: Every time I sneeze I have an orgasm.

Second girl: What are you taking for it?

First girl: Snuff.

How does a Hollywood wife pick her nose?
From a catalogue.

Why does it take a woman with PMT twenty minutes to iron a shirt?
BECAUSE IT JUST DOES.

What do you call a lady Sloane Ranger working in a law office?
The caterer.

Three nuns go to confession.
The first nun said, 'Forgive me, oh Father, but I looked at a man's privates.'
'Go and wash your eyes with Holy Water,' said the priest.
The second nun went in.
'Forgive me, Oh Father, I touched a man's privates.'
'Go and wash your hands in the holy water.'
Finally the third nun came out of confession and said to the others, 'Move over sisters, I gotta gargle.'

There was a young woman who was desperately unhappy because she was so flat-chested. Her cries were so anguished that they reached the ears of her fairy godmother who appeared and offered to grant her one wish.

'Oh, easy,' said the girl, 'I want a large chest.'

'All right,' said the fairy, 'from now on, every time a man says pardon to you, your bosoms will grow.'

The next day, the girl was walking down a street when a man bumped into her.

'Oh, I beg your pardon,' he said.

She was delighted to see that her bosom grew an inch.

The following week, she was at the supermarket and another man bumped into her.

'Oh, pardon,' he said.

Her chest grew another inch and she was more than happy with the way things were going.

That night she went out for a Chinese dinner and a waiter accidentally spilled some food on her lap.

He bowed and said, 'A thousand pardons, I beg you.'

The next morning the headlines of the local paper ran: CHINESE WAITER KILLED BY TWO MYSTERY TORPEDOES.

Why are dumb blondes only allowed a half-hour lunch?

So their bosses don't have to retrain them in the afternoon.

What does a Jewish American princess make for dinner?

Reservations.

A man in a park ran to the park keeper crying, 'Quick, come here, I think a man is making love to a dead body.'

The park keeper ran over to sort out the situation but returned moments later sighing with relief.

'She's not dead, sir,' he said, 'she's English.'

What do you get when you turn three blondes upside down?

Two brunettes.

What's black and white and tells the Pope to f**ck himself?

A nun who's just won the lottery.

'Every night my wife covers her face in a mud pack and puts her hair in rollers.

'Does it help?'

'A little. But I can still tell it's her.'

What does an Essex girl use for protection during sex?

A bus shelter.

What do Sloane Rangers say to men they fancy?

Would you like to give one one?

What do Sloane Rangers use that are six inches long and buzz?

Mobile phones.

A nun went into an off licence and asked for a bottle of whisky.

'Whisky?' the assistant asked. 'I thought you nun's didn't drink.'

'We don't,' the nun replied, 'this is for the Mother Superior's constipation.'

She bought the whisky and left.

Later that night, the assistant saw the same nun dead drunk on a park bench.

'I thought that was for the Mother Superior's constipation?' he said.

'It ish,' she replied. 'When she sees me like this, she'll shit herself.'

Marriage councillor: Are your relations pleasant?

Woman: Mine are, his are horrid.

What do you say to an Essex girl who can suck a golf ball through a hose pipe?

Marry me.

Kate and Maureen, two nymphomaniacs, promised each other that if one died she would come back and tell the other what it was like beyond the grave.

Kate died and after a few weeks made contact with her old friend Maureen.

'So what's it like?' Maureen asked.

'Well,' said Kate, 'the sun shines all day. I get up in the morning, have a light breakfast then a little sex. Then another little snack and some more sex. Then a small lunch and more sex and a snooze in the sun.'

'Wow,' said Maureen, 'heaven sounds great.'

'Heaven?' Kate exclaimed. 'I'm not in heaven. I'm a rabbit in the Arizona desert.'

What's an Essex girl's favourite cigarette?

More.

Roses are red
Violets are blue
Your mother's a cracker
What happened to you?

'I've been married twice,' said one man to another.

'Divorced, huh?' said the other.

'Nope,' he said sadly. 'My first wife died of mushroom poisoning. And my second wife died of a fractured skull.'

'How awful,' said the second man. 'How did she fracture her skull?'

'Wouldn't eat her mushrooms.'

A widow whose singular vice
Was to keep her late husband on ice,
Said, 'It's hard since I lost him
I'll never defrost him
Cold comfort but cheap at the price.'

Two women meet at a party.

First woman: We've met before actually. At the Brenman's five years ago.

Second woman: Really? You obviously have quite a memory.

First woman: Not really. I'm hopeless at names, but I never forget a dress.

Three pregnant woman were having a check-up. The doctor asked the first woman what position she conceived in.

'He was on top,' she replied.

'Then you will have a boy!' the doctor proclaimed.

The second woman was asked the same question.

'I was on top,' she said.

'Then you will have a girl!' said the doctor.

With this the third woman burst into tears.

'What's the matter?' asked the doctor.

'Am I going to have puppies. . . ?'

There was a young lady of Wantage
Of whom the Town Clerk took advantage.
Said the County Surveyor,
'Of course you must pay her
You've altered the line of her frontage.'

Why did the Essex girl go up on the roof?
    She heard that the drinks were on the house.

How do you make a bimbo's eyes light up?
    Shine a torch in her ear.

What's the mating cry of a dumb blonde?
    I'm SOOOooooo drunk.

SHE: I've just come from the beauty parlour.
    HE: Closed, huh?

What's big and pink and too hard for a Sloane Ranger in the morning?
The Financial Times.

A woman went into a shop and said, 'I'd like to try that dress on in the window.'

'Well madam,' replied the shop assistant, 'I'm afraid you'll have to try it on in the dressing room like everyone else.'

What do Essex girls have written on their underwear?
Next.

In a survey carried out to see what men like about women, thirty per cent said they liked fat legs, twenty percent said they liked slim legs and fifty per cent said they liked something in between.

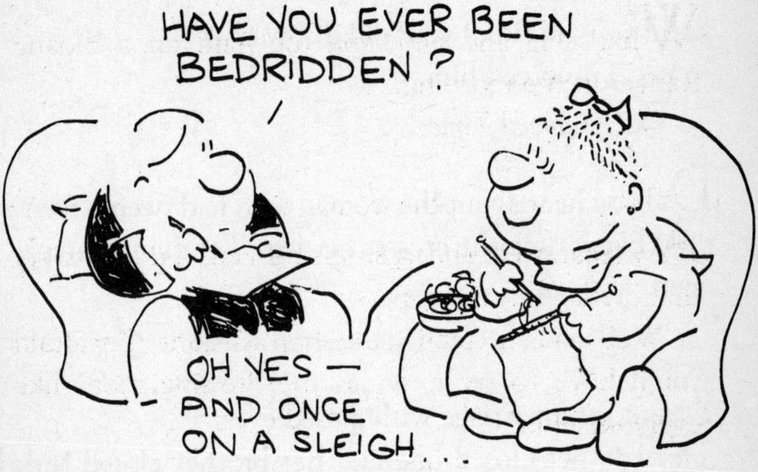
HAVE YOU EVER BEEN BEDRIDDEN?
OH YES — AND ONCE ON A SLEIGH...

Did you get rid of your old dishwasher?
  Yes. I divorced him.

Did you hear about the woman who had twenty face lifts? Every time she crosses her legs, her mouth snaps open.

I went into marriage with closed eyes.
  Her father closed one and her brother closed the other.

Why can't a woman with a wooden leg give change for a pound note?
  Because she's only got half a knicker.

What is the only thing that a Jewish American princess will go down on?
  The escalator at Bloomingdales.

A woman came home from a party complaining about one of the guests.

'She must have yawned about fifty times while I was talking to her.'

'Maybe she wasn't yawning,' suggested her husband. 'Maybe she was trying to say something.'

What's the definition of a flirt?
A girl who thinks it's every man for herself.

When a Spanish wife discovered that her husband had a mistress, all hell broke loose. To get out of it, he explained to her that as his main rival had a mistress, he had to have one too.

Some weeks later, the couple were out at the ballet. The husband pointed out his rival and his mistress two rows in front.

'And sitting in front of them,' he explained, 'is my mistress.'

'Really?' exclaimed the wife. 'I think ours is the much prettier of the two.'

Two girls were talking one day. One said that her boyfriend had a dandruff problem but she gave him 'Head and Shoulders' and it cleared up.

'How do you give shoulders?' asked the other.

My mother-in-law almost broke up our marriage.

One day my wife came home early and found me in bed with her.

Why do dumb blondes hate Smarties?

They're too hard to peel.

How can you tell if your secretary is an Essex girl?

Tippex marks all over the computer screen.

What did the English woman reply when asked if she was sexually active?

'No. I just lie there.'

Why is virginity like a balloon?
One prick and it's gone.

'I don't know what all this fuss is about weight. My wife lost two stone last year when swimming. Mind you, I don't know how she did it. I tied them round her neck securely enough.'

What does wife stand for?
Washing, ironing, f***ing, etc.

A man was going in for a sex change and his friend asked him if he was scared.
'It isn't the pain of having my balls removed I fear,' he replied, 'as much as having my mouth stretched and my brain shrunk.'

How do you tell the Irish bride at a wedding?
She's the one in a maternity dress.

How many feminists does it take to change a light-bulb?

One. And that's NOT FUNNY.

How do you tell an Italian movie star from an American one?

She's the one with the moustache.

What's the definition of a nymphomaniac?

A girl who will go to bed with a man even after she's just had her hair done.

What does a dumb blonde say after sex?

'Say . . . who are you guys anyway?'

What's the definition of a nymphomaniac?

A girl who trips you up and is under you before you hit the floor.

A white woman went into a porn shop and asked, 'How much for the white dildo?'

'Fifteen pounds,' answered the sales assistant.

'And how much for the black one?'

'Same price,' came the answer.

'I think I'll take the black one. I've never tried one of those before.'

An hour later, a black woman came in and asked the same questions.

'Then I think I'll take the white one. I've never tried one of those before.'

An hour later, a young blonde comes in and asks about the white and black dildos.

'Fifteen pounds each,' said the assistant.

'And what about the plaid one?' she asked looking up at the top shelf.

'Oh that's a very special one,' said the assistant. 'Thirty-five pounds.'

She thought for a moment then said, 'OK I'll take the plaid one. I've never tried one of those before.'

An hour later, the owner of the shop came by. 'How's it going?' he asked.

'Good,' said the assistant. 'I sold two dildos, a black one and a white one. Oh, and I sold your thermos flask for thirty-five pounds.'

How do you make a feminist smile?
Shove a coat hanger in her mouth.

There once was a girl from Cape Cod
Who dreamt she'd been jumped on by God
But 'tweren't the Almighty
That lifted her nightie
But Roger, the lodger, the sod.

What's the definition of gross ignorance?
144 blondes.

What do you call four blondes lying on the ground?
An air mattress.

A friend told a housewife it would cut down on the housework if she used paper plates.

'I tried it,' she complained, 'but they clog up my dishwasher.'

What do you call an Essex girl with two 'O' levels?
A liar.

An old lady went into a shop and asked the price of grade 'A' eggs.

'Two pounds a dozen,' said the shop assistant.
'And the grade 'B's?'
'One pound fifty.'
'And cracked eggs?'
'Fifty pence.'
'OK then,' she said, 'crack me a dozen grade 'A's.'

How does a bimbo hold her liquor?
By the ears.

FIRST WOMAN: Do you get your good looks from your mother or your father?

SECOND WOMAN: My father. He's a plastic surgeon.

A woman was serving on a jury and chose to acquit a woman who had obviously murdered her husband.

'Why?' asked a journalist later.

'I felt sorry for her,' said the woman. 'She was a widow.'

How can you tell a bimbo's boyfriend?

He's the one with the belt buckle that matches the impression in her forehead.

How does a Jewish American princess call her children down for dinner?

'Taxi's here.'

A man who had just inherited a lot of money was about to marry a beautiful model but he was having doubts about her sincerity.

'Are you marrying me because my uncle died and left me three million dollars?' he asked.

'No, of course not,' she replied. 'I'd marry you no matter who'd left it to you.'

A lady driver was bragging to her friends that she always drove with the emergency brake on.

'But why?' asked one of them.

'So if an emergency happens, I'm ready,' she answered.

A woman went to see her solicitor and told him she wanted a divorce.

'On what grounds?' he asked.

'He's unfaithful,' she replied.

'What makes you think that?' he asked.

'I don't think he's the father of my child,' she said.

A new bride knitted a sweater for her husband who was in the army and stationed abroad. When she sent it, she enclosed a note:

Dear John,

I knitted this myself but the airmail stamps were so expensive that I've had to cut off all the buttons to make the parcel lighter.

Love Jess

P.S. You'll find the buttons in the right-hand pocket.

What did Sir Lancelot ask Lady Guinevere?

Who was that last knight I saw you with, lady?

An American woman at a UN cocktail party had asked a diplomat, 'What 'nese are you – Japanese, Chinese or Javanese?'

'I happen to be Japanese, madam,' he said in impeccable English. 'And what 'kee are you. Monkee, donkee or Yankee?'

Did you hear about the girl that was so thin she had tattooed on her chest: 'In case of sex, this side up'?

Immediately after the first act of a play, Bernadette wanted to leave the theatre and go and have a drink.

'But don't you want to stay for the second half?' asked her friend.

'We've loads of time yet,' said Bernadette. 'The programme says the second act takes place three weeks later.'

What does an Essex girl put behind her ears to make her more attractive?

Her feet.

There's only one thing more expensive than a wife.

What's that?

An ex wife.

My wife's cooking is so bad, we give the leftovers to the dog. And he gives them to the cat.

A man and his wife were rowing in a restaurant. The man screamed, 'You cow. Of all the low-down, low-life bitches, you're the worst. You're a miserable excuse for a human being.'

The wife was just about to launch into him in reply when she realised everyone in the place was listening.

'Quite right darling,' she said, 'and then what did you say to her?'

SHE: I come from a hunting family. My mother has gone out hunting every day for years now.

HE: Really. Hunting what?

SHE: My father.

My wife doesn't need to call us for dinner. We just listen for the smoke alarm.

What's the definition of a nervous woman?
One who has to have two stiff gins to give her the courage to open her bottle of tranquillisers.

*Little Mary pinned her hopes
On a book by Marie Stopes.
Judging by the girl's condition
It must have been an old edition.*

What do you call women who use the rhythm method?
Mothers.

My wife has two complaints:
One that she has nothing to wear. And two, that she's run out of wardrobe space to keep it in.

She has her husband eating out of her hand. She says it saves on the washing up.

How many Jewish mothers does it take to change a light-bulb?

None. I'll just sit here in the dark, on my own, alone in the dark, as usual.

HE: What do virgins eat for breakfast?
SHE: I don't know.
HE: I thought so.

FIRST MAN: I wanted to marry her but her family objected.
SECOND MAN: Her family?
FIRST MAN: Yes. Her husband and their three kids.

FIRST MAN: Isn't that suit too big for you?
SECOND MAN: Yes, but it was a present from my wife and I didn't want to hurt her feelings. One day I got home early and there it was, folded on the end of the bed.

How does an Essex girl turn on the light after sex?
Kicks the car door open.

SHE: How strange! You look like my third husband.
HE: Third! How many have you had?
SHE: Two.

Bert was waiting for his blind date at the cinema when a girl walked past him.
BERT: Are you Mary?
GIRL: Are you Bert?
BERT: Yes.
GIRL: Then I'm not Mary.

WOMAN: Can I have some more sleeping tablets for my husband?
DOCTOR: Why? Is he having trouble sleeping?
WOMAN: No, he's woken up.

What's the definition of a modest woman?

One who pulls down the shades before she changes her mind.

What do you call a fly buzzing about in a dumb blonde's head?

A space invader.

What's the difference between being a wife in the East and in the West?

In the East you often don't see your husband before the wedding. In the West you often don't see him afterwards.

A wife took her husband to marriage guidance counselling.

'What's the problem?' asked the councillor.

'What's his name here thinks I don't pay him enough attention,' complained the woman.

HE: Darling. What's this on my plate?
  SHE: Why?
  HE: In case I have to describe it to the doctor.

I said to my mother-in-law, 'Our house is your house.'
Last week she sold it.

A Jewish mother brought her son two silk ties, a green one and a red one. On the night of his birthday, he came down wearing the green one.
  'So vat's vrong with the red one?' she asked.

My wife never knows what she wants until the next-door neighbour gets it.

What do you see when you look deeply into a dumb blonde's eyes?
  The back of her head.

H<small>E</small>: I've never seen you put down the phone so fast. It was only ten minutes.

S<small>HE</small>: It was a wrong number.

D<small>id</small> you hear about the bride who got married in her grandmother's dress? She looked wonderful but her grandmother froze to death.

W<small>hy</small> does a dumb blonde have TGIF painted on her shoes?

Toes go in first.

A<small></small> man wasn't well so his wife took him to the doctor. After the examination, the doctor asked her to come in.

'Your husband needs more sex. I'm prescribing it three times a week from now on.'

'OK,' she said, 'put me down for every other Tuesday.'

A young girl saw her parents making love one evening in their bedroom. The next day she asked her father if they had been wrestling.

'Oh no,' said the father, 'your mother was having a fit and I was holding her down.'

A few days later when the father came home after work, his daughter ran to him crying, 'Dad, Dad. Mum had another of those fits today and the milkman had to hold her down for ages.'

A wife on her deathbed called for her husband. She begged him to forgive her as she had been unfaithful and had many lovers while all the time he had been so kind and good.

'Don't feel bad,' he said. 'That's why I poisoned you.'

Why do bimbos like cars with sun roofs?

More leg room.

A bride was wearing very elegant but very tight shoes for her wedding. That night, when she started to undress, try as she might, she couldn't get them off.

The groom pulled as much as he could to help but even he couldn't get them off.

'We'll have to use a knife,' he said.

'No! NO!' cried the voice of her mother from the room next door. 'Try butter first.'

FIRST WOMAN: Why are you getting divorced?

SECOND WOMAN: My husband's careless about his appearance. He hasn't shown up for three years.

If a woman with briefs is a lawyer, what is a woman without briefs?

A solicitor.

How do you know when an Essex girl is having an orgasm?

She drops her kebab.

A mother found her daughter still in bed one morning.

'Come on get up and get ready for school.'

'No,' said the daughter. 'I'm not going.'

'You must go,' said the mother.

'Shan't. I've got my reasons.'

'OK,' said the mother, 'give me two good reasons why you shouldn't go.'

'Well, first the children don't like me. And second, neither do the teachers.'

'That makes no difference,' argued her mother, 'you must still go.'

'OK then, give me two good reasons why I should go.'

'Well,' said the mother, 'first you're forty-five years old. And second, you're the headmistress.'

FIRST WOMAN: How do you keep your youth?
SECOND WOMAN: I lock him in the wardrobe.

How does an Essex girl avoid headaches?
Buys padded dashboards.

Why is a bimbo like a door knob?
Because everyone gets a turn.

My wife has found the best way to avoid bad smells in the kitchen. She doesn't cook.

Why is a blonde bimbo like a railroad track?
Because she gets laid all over the country.

BRIDE-TO-BE: I want the wedding to be perfect, Mum, so we mustn't overlook even the most insignificant detail.
MOTHER: Oh don't worry. I'm sure he'll show up.

Did you hear about the woman who ran out of ice cubes? She couldn't make any more because she'd lost the recipe.

A journalist was asking women on the street which woman they most admired. She got all sorts of replies: Golda Meir, Brigitte Bardot, Margaret Thatcher, Elizabeth Hurley, Kylie . . .

One foreign woman, however, answered Alaska Pippalinié.

'I've never heard of her,' said the journalist. 'Who's Alaska Pippalinié?'

'I read about her in the paper,' replied the woman. 'She made the headlines. "Alaska Pipeline laid by five hundred men in six months." Wouldn't you like to have her life?'

HE: Am I the first man to make love to you?
  SHE: You could be. Your face does look familiar.

What do you say to a bimbo who won't give in?
Have another beer.

What's a bimbo's favourite nursery rhyme?
Humpme Dumpme

Three women, one French, one Italian and one English, were discussing their sex lives.

The French woman said, 'My 'usband ee come home, ee kiss my ear, nibble my neck then make love to me. It drive me wild.'

The second woman said.

'My 'usband ee bring me flowers, ee bring me perfume. Ee nibble my toes, ee kiss my hands, ee kiss me all over then he make love to me. It drive me completely wild.'

They turned to the English woman and asked what drove her man in bed.

'Our Ted gets 'ome. He 'as his chips an steak. He 'as a brew, reads t'paper then we go upstairs and he has his way with me. Then after, 'e wipes his dick on the duvet. Drives me flaming bonkers.'

Why are women such bad parkers?

Because they're always being told that two inches is six.

A woman was on the phone to her friend.

'That husband of mine's a liar,' she said. 'He says he spent the night with Dave.'

'Perhaps he did,' said her friend.

'I know he didn't,' insisted the woman.

'But how?'

'Because I did.'

HUSBAND: If I died would you marry again?

WIFE: I suppose so.

HUSBAND: Would you make love to him?

WIFE: Suppose so.

HUSBAND: Would you give him my clothes?

WIFE: No chance. He's not your size.

FIRST MAN: My wife gave me a really unusual birthday present.

SECOND MAN: What?

FIRST MAN: She let me win an argument.

What's the definition of old age?

When all the numbers in her little black book are doctors.

A woman entered a police station to report her husband missing.

'Can you describe him?' says the officer in charge.

'Tall, dark, athletic looking, blue eyes.'

Another officer overheard and said, 'Wait a minute, I know your husband. He's nothing like that.'

'I know,' said the woman, 'but who wants that same old jerk back?'

'Mum what is a grey hair a sign of?'

'The beautician going on holiday.'

What does a bimbo do when someone shouts 'there's a mouse in the room?'

Checks her highlights.

A young wife came home to find her mother in the kitchen with her husband, Mark. Her mother was standing on a chair with her feet in a bucket of water. She had one finger in a light socket and two wires connected to either side of her head. Mark was just about to switch on the electric supply.

Her mother waved gaily and said, 'Darling. You're just in time to see Mark cure my rheumatism.'

How do blonde brain cells die?
Alone.

What do you call a blonde with two brain cells?
Pregnant.

What's the difference between a bride and groom?
The bride looks stunning and the groom looks stunned.

A woman went to see her doctor.

'It's my mother you see, I think she's gone senile,' she said.

'What makes you think that?' asked the doctor.

'Well, she thinks she's a washing machine. She sits in the corner rolling her eyes, gurgling . . .'

'That's awful,' said the doctor. 'What do you want me to do?'

'Perhaps have a gentle word. You see, she's not very good with the woollens.'

HUSBAND: Is this coffee or tea? It tastes like turpentine.

WIFE: Must be tea. My coffee tastes like lighter fluid.

What's the definition of a well-balanced woman?

One that can cook like her mother and drink like her father.

My wife's dinners melt in the mouth. I wish she'd defrost them first.

An old lady was feeling unwell so she went to the doctor. He examined her and asked her to keep a record of what she passed.

The next day she was feeling better when she saw him so he asked, 'Did you pass anything out of the ordinary?'

'Not really,' she replied, 'a dog, a cat and two foreigners on bicycles.'

'Well,' he said, astonished, 'no wonder you're feeling better.'

Her face looked like a million. All green and wrinkled.

What's the definition of a gossip?

A woman who has a good sense of rumour.

WHAT DID YOU LEARN ON YOUR FIRST DAY AT SCHOOL, LITTLE PRECIOUS?
PRECIOUS LITTLE...

WOMAN: Doctor, I have a small embarrassing wart.
   DOCTOR: So divorce him.

'It's true,' confessed Jane, Lady Torres
That often I beg lifts in lorries.
When men stop to piss
I see things that I miss
When travelling alone in my Morris.

'What's the gadget that does all the housework
called?'
   'A wife.'

What's the definition of mixed emotion?
   When your mother-in-law drives off a cliff in your
new car.

What did the Essex girl think *coq au vin* was?
   Sex in a lorry.

He: What did you hear at the opera last night?

She: Oh all sorts, the Brenmans are bankrupt, The Fords are getting divorced and Pete Robinson has run off with his secretary.

What's the difference between a woman with PMT and the KGB?

You can reason with the KGB.

Husband: Darling. What's your favourite sexual position?

Wife: Next door.

My doctor put me on a diet.

Oh what can you have?

Three males a day.

Why aren't bimbos good cattle herders?

Because they can't even keep two calves together.

She was only the Town Clerk's daughter but she let the borough surveyor.

A dumb blonde was stopped for speeding and taken down to the local police station.

The officer in charge got up and unzipped his trousers.

'Oh no,' said the girl, 'not another breathalyser test.'

What's the difference between sleeping with an Essex girl and the Starship enterprise?

The Starship goes where no man has been before.

Two women were chatting.

'Have I got a sore throat,' moaned one.

'When I have a sore throat I suck on a Life Saver,' said the other.

'Easy for you. You live at the beach.'

What do you call a girl who has just been run over by a car?
Patty.

What's 10, 9, 8, 7, 6, 5, 4, 3, 2, 1?
Bo Derek getting older.

What's the difference between a job you hate and a wife?
After five years, the job still sucks.

Why do some women prefer sex to bowling?
The balls are lighter and you don't have to change your shoes.

What do you call a Sloane Ranger working in a stockbroker's office?
The interior decorator.

Once, during the Christmas holiday, the Bionic woman took an overnight train journey. She went to her berth, not noticing that a man was in the lower bunk.

As she undressed, he peeked through the curtains to watch her. She took off her wig, a glass eye, her mechanical hand, a bionic leg.

Suddenly she saw him and shrieked, 'What do you want?'

'I think you know,' he said. 'Now unscrew it and toss it down here.'

Two girls are talking about men and one is being a bit superior about the fact that she plays hard to get.

'For instance,' she said, 'I didn't accept Clive the first time he proposed.'

'I know,' the other replied. 'you weren't there.'

I bought my mother-in-law a lovely chair for her birthday. Trouble is, my wife won't let me plug it in.

A prissy spinster phoned the police station to complain about a nude man that she could see from her flat. A policeman came to investigate. 'Why,' he said, 'you can't even see his window from here.'

'Try standing on the table and looking down through the skylight,' the woman replied.

The morning after:

ITALIAN WOMAN: Now you will never respect me.

AMERICAN WOMAN: Who the hell are you? I must have been stoned.

GERMAN WOMAN: Voud you like zum sausages and zum beer?

SWEDISH WOMAN: I go for shower now an then go home.

FRENCH WOMAN: Do I get new outfit for this, oui?

JEWISH WOMAN: I should have held out for a new coat or at least a ring.

ENGLISH WOMAN: There dear. Does it all feel better now?

What do you call a woman who always knows where her husband is?

A widow.

A Jewish girl rings her parents from college.

'Guess what Ma, I'm getting married.'

'Why, that's wonderful dear.'

'But he's not Jewish.'

'So, I bet he's a nice boy if you picked him. What does he do?'

'He doesn't work Ma, he's had a bit of a problem with drugs in the past but he hopes to be in a rock band some day.'

'Well I'm sure he's a nice boy. And where will you live?'

'Well we were wondering if we could stay with you?'

'Sure you can have our room, your dad'll sleep on the sofa till you're settled.'

'But Ma, where will you sleep?'

'Me? Don't worry about me. I'm gonna drop dead as soon as you put down the phone.'

Did you hear about the Eskimo girl who spent the night with her boyfriend?

The next morning she found out she was six months pregnant.

Ages of women:

16–25: like Africa – partly explored, partly virgin territory

25–35: like the Far East – hot and mysterious

35–45: like Europe – worn but interesting in parts

45–55: like America – willing to experiment but partly plastic

55–65: like Russia – had her years of glory in days gone by

65—: like the Arctic – everyone knows where it is but no one wants to go there.

It took time but Harry eventually developed an attachment for his mother-in-law.

It fitted over her mouth.

One afternoon, a doctor saw a stunning looking girl waiting in his surgery. She was the last of his patients to be called into his office. He asked her to lie on his examination couch but found he couldn't resist her and start to kiss her neck.

'Do you know what I am doing?' he asked.

'Oh yes,' she said, 'looking for thyroid trouble, inflamed glands, ear problems . . .'

Then he started to feel her breasts.

'Do you know what I am doing now?'

'Oh yes,' she said, 'checking for chest problems, skin infections, any growths . . .'

Then he moved his hand to her stomach which he caressed. 'And now?'

'Oh, checking for swelling, possible liver problems, appendicitis?'

The doctor couldn't hold back anymore. He jumped on top of her and started to make love to her.

'And now,' he panted, 'what am I doing now?'

'Getting the clap,' she said. 'That's what I came in to see you about.'

A couple weren't talking to each other and were communicating through notes. One night, the wife went to bed and there pinned on her husband's back was a note saying, 'Wake me at seven.'

The next day, he awoke at nine thirty, and realised he'd overslept. Pinned to his back was a note saying, 'Wake up, it's seven o'clock.'

Two nosey Catholic women were chatting and looking out of the window at a house opposite which was owned by a call girl.

In the morning, they saw a Protestant minister go in.

'Shocking,' they said, tut-tutting away.

In the afternoon, a rabbi went in.

'Disgraceful,' they said, 'what ever is the world coming to?'

In the evening, a priest went in.

'To be sure,' said one, 'the poor girl must be really ill.'

A wife was nervous about her first driving lessons.

'I don't know what to do,' she said to her husband.

'Easy,' he said, 'just pretend you're in the back and I'm driving.'

A young woman was giving details of a car accident that she was in.

'And what gear were you in at the time of the accident?' asked the police officer.

'Oh a little peach off-the-shoulder number with matching shoes and pearls,' she replied.

What's the difference between a bimbo and Mars?

There may be intelligent life on Mars.

A man took his girlfriend to a Chinese restaurant. When the waiter came to ask how she'd like her rice – boiled, fried or steamed – she looked at the man and said pointedly 'thrown'.

My wife does bird imitations.
She watches me like a hawk.

What do you call a woman who does chores for a hundred pounds a week?
A cleaner.
What do you call a woman who does it for nothing?
Married.

Two girls were forced to share a room as the hotel was full. After they had checked in one said to the other, 'There's something I have to tell you about myself. I want to be frank . . .'
'No,' interrupted the other, '*I* want to be Frank.'

Three old ladies were sitting in the park when a man came by and flashed at them.
Two of them had a stroke, the third wasn't fast enough.

A very demanding and critical wife got home one day after a long trip.

'How's my cat?' she asked her husband.

'Dead,' said her husband.

'For God's sake,' she shrieked, 'is that any way to tell me? What you should have done is broken it more gently, said she was playing on the roof when she slipped and injured herself and you took her to the vet where she passed away quietly. By the way, how's my mother?'

'Well,' said her husband, 'she was playing on the roof . . .'

What's a brunette's mating call?

'Has that blonde gone yet?'

What's the difference between a Sloane Ranger and an Essex girl?

Sloane Rangers have real jewellery and fake orgasms.

A wife suspected her husband of playing around so when they were invited to a fancy dress party she had a plan to trap him. She feigned a headache and he went alone, dressed as a gorilla.

Later she donned a disguise of her own and went to the party, where she saw her husband flirting with every woman in the room. She approached him, flirted with him herself and eventually enticed him upstairs where she seduced him.

Just before the unmasking at midnight, she drove home. The next morning she confronted her husband.

'How was the party?' she said.

'Oh, I had to get rid of that gorilla costume, I was too hot in it. Old Harwood wore it, though, and said he had the time of his life.'

A young woman went to the chemist to buy some talcum powder. The chemist, who was very bow-legged, said, 'Certainly madam, walk this way.'

'If I could walk that way,' said the woman, 'I wouldn't need the talcum powder.'

A wife found out her husband had a mistress and she decided to ask what this woman had that she hadn't.

'Well,' he said, 'to tell the truth, you're cold and unresponsive, whereas my mistress groans and moans with real feeling when I'm with her.'

Fine, she thinks, I could do that.

The next evening she seduces him and half-way through she remembers what he said and decides to give it her best shot:

'I've had a terrible day today, I came out of the supermarket, it's raining, I wait for a bus, none come, then what do you know? Three come all at once and not one a twenty-three.'

What does an Essex girl shout at a rugby match when Wayne yells, 'great tackle'?

'Yeah an' a neat arse, too.'

Marriage is a three-ring game. First the engagement ring, second the wedding ring, third the suffer ring.

Two women were talking in a café.

'I got so excited the other day,' said one, 'I thought I'd lost one hundred and sixty pounds of ugly fat. But he came home.'

A man and his beautiful wife were in a car crash and his wife's face was badly scarred. The doctor told him he could repair her face but he would need to graft some new skin on, which he could take from the husband's behind.

The operation was carried out and was a great success.

'Didn't it hurt?' asked a friend.

'Sure,' the man said, 'but it's worth it for the pleasure I get every time my wife's mother kisses her daughter and I know she's kissing my arse.'

What's the difference between an Essex girl and a supermarket trolley?

The supermarket trolley has a mind of its own.

Three weeks before the birth of her baby a woman visited her gynaecologist.

'How should I lie to give birth?' she asked.

'In the position you were in at the time of conception,' reassured the doctor.

'What!' said the woman, 'in the back of the car with my legs out the window?'

A professor was lecturing about birthday statistics.

'Somewhere in the world a woman is giving birth every minute,' he said, 'day and night. What should we do about it?'

'Find her,' said one of the audience, 'and stop her.'

There once was a young girl called Rhoda,
Who constructed herself a pagoda.
And the walls of the halls
Were festooned with the balls
And the tools of the fools who bestrode her.

What are the seven ages of a woman?
Her own and six guesses.

At a party, a well stacked girl was wearing a chain with a tiny aeroplane on it. One of the guests, a young man, kept staring at it.

'Do you like my aeroplane?' she asked.

'Yes,' he replied, 'but not half as much as the landing field.'

What do you call a dumb blonde at a university?
A visitor.

Two plastic surgeons were talking about a client who was suing one of them.

'You can't win,' the unlucky one said, 'she's had so many face lifts, I had no choice.'

'So what exactly is she suing you for?' his colleague asked.

'The fact that she's got a beard now,' he replied.

How do you know when a Jewish American princess
has had an orgasm?
   She drops her nail file.

Jack and Jill went up the hill
to fetch a pail of water.
Jill forgot to take her pill
And now she's got a daughter.

A woman's best beauty aid is a short-sighted man.

Why are girls called birds?
   Because they pick up men.

A woman in Las Vegas was running up and down the
street putting money in the parking meters. When a
passer-by asked her what she was doing, she replied:
   'Outdoor gambling.'

A Spanish girl called Carmen married a Jew called Hymie Cohen. She wanted to remain a good Catholic but she also wanted to support her husband's religion, so she decided on a compromise. She attended synagogue on Saturday and church on Sunday. Trouble was, at the weekend she didn't know whether she was Carmen or Cohen.

Twenty-five is a nice age for a woman . . . especially if she's forty.

She was only the admiral's daughter, but she loved a naval encounter.

There was a young lady from Louth
Who suddenly grew very stout.
Her mother said 'Nelly,
There's more in your belly,
Than ever went into your mouth.'

She was only the mayor of Birmingham's daughter, but she knew five ways.

What's a Jewish American princess's idea of sexual compatibility?
    Simultaneous headaches.

There was a young girl from Darjeeling
Who could dance with such exquisite feeling,
There was never a sound
For miles around
Save of fly buttons hitting the ceiling.

FIRST MAN: I got this bottle of sherry for my mother-in-law.
    SECOND MAN: What a great exchange!

Women like the simple things in life . . . like men.

There was a young girl of La Plata
Who was widely known as a farter.
Her deafening reports
At the Argentine Sports
Made her much in demand as a starter.

FIRST MAN: It's unlucky to see the bride the night before the wedding.

SECOND MAN: And sometimes for thirty years afterwards.

HE: I see that your birthday is on 25 March. May I ask which year?

SHE: Every year.

FIRST MAN: I decided it was time to tell my wife who was the boss.

SECOND MAN: Good for you. What did you say?

FIRST MAN: You're the boss.

Her age is a millinery secret. She keeps it under her hat.

She was an amazing woman. She had everything a man could ever want – big muscles, a beard and a moustache.

What's the definition of a snob?
  A woman who has monogrammed tea bags.

Mary had a little lamb. The midwife was treated for shock.

There was a young lady from France,
Who decided to just take a chance.
For a hour or so
She let herself go
And now all her sisters are aunts.

She was only the groom's daughter, but all the horse manure.

She was only the road maker's daughter, but she liked her asphalt.

There was a young lady of Rheims
Who amazingly pissed in four streams.
A friend poked around,
A coat button was found
Wedged tightly in one of her seams.

What's an Essex girl's favourite hymn?
  'O Come all ye faithful'.

WOMAN: Do you think I'll lose my looks when I'm older?
  MAN: Only if you're lucky.

My wife loves me so much. Last month when I was home ill, every time a tradesman came to the door, even if it was only the milkman, she'd run down the path crying, 'My husband's home, my husband's home'.

FIRST MAN: My mother-in-law has parrot's disease.
SECOND MAN: Sorry to hear that. Is it serious?
FIRST MAN: Yes, she repeats everything she hears.

On the chest of a barmaid in Sale
Was tattooed the price of the ale
And on her behind
For the sake of the blind
Was the same information in Braille.

FIRST MAN: Did the mud pack improve your wife's appearance?
SECOND MAN: Yes, until it fell off.

Three women were complaining about their sex lives.

'My husband's ninety-five. He's far too old to do it anymore,' said the first.

'My husband prefers men,' said the second.

They turned to the third wife, who was married to a TV presenter.

'No better,' she sighed. 'All he ever does is sit on the end of the bed and tell me how good it's going to be.'

There was a young lady of Tottenham
Who'd no manners, or else she'd forgotten 'em.
At tea at the vicar's
She tore off her knickers
Because, she explained, she felt hot in 'em.

What's the the definition of a woman who balances her finances?

One who pays her Visa card bills with her American Express.

Give a woman an inch and she thinks she's a ruler.

Behind every great woman there's a man who's let her down.

An unhappy bride went to the doctor to complain about her husband's sexual technique. The doctor advised her to tell her husband what she wanted in bed.

That night, she said to her husband, 'Put your hand on my breast and say "I love you".'

He did.

'Lower,' she murmured.

'I love you,' he said gruffly.

Mary had a little lamb
With which she used to sleep.
Too late she found it was a ram
And now she has a little lamb.

She was only the newsagent's daughter, but she sure loved her *Daily Mail*.

She was only the cab driver's daughter, but you sure auto meter.

Little Bo Peep
Has lost her sheep,
They were eaten by a leopard.
But what she really meant to keep
Was taken by the shepherd.

What's a Jewish American princess's definition of natural childbirth?
   Absolutely no make-up.

Marriage is the process of finding out what kind of husband your wife would have preferred.

Why is eating out with a bimbo like committing a crime?

Crime never pays either.

A woman who strives to be like a man lacks ambition.

FIRST MAN: I hate my mother-in-law.

SECOND MAN: But without her you wouldn't have met your wife.

FIRST MAN: Exactly.

Lil went out with many men.
And accepted all they gave her.
But she married a man with a will of his own.
Made out in her favour.

An older man gave his young girlfriend a skunk coat.

'Wow!' she said. 'It's amazing that such a gorgeous coat could come from such a smelly little beast.'

'Hey,' said the man, 'there's no need to get personal!'

A small boy who was watching his mother do the dishes asked her:

'Where did you work before you got the job with us?'

What's the difference between before and after marriage?

Before she tells him where to take her, after she tells him where to go.

There was a young girl of Australia
Who painted her arse as a dahlia.
The drawing was fine
And the colour divine
But the scent on the whole was a failure.

Why do women like the English cricket team so much?

They stay on top for two days but come second in the end.

There was a young lady of Wylde
Who kept herself quite undefiled
By thinking of Jesus,
Contagious diseases
And the bother of having a child.

Did you hear about the dumb blonde who thought that intercourse was the time spent between classes?

She thought that a mushroom was a place for love.

Darling Reggie

I've been distraught since that stupid quarrel last week. Let's put it all behind us and kiss and make up. Throwing my engagement ring at you was a ridiculous thing to do. I hope you realise how much I really treasure it and will give it back to me. I've said a lot of silly things that I didn't mean. I won't sleep or eat until I've heard from you.

Please call me, my only, my love.

Yours forever,

Dora

PS Congratulations on winning the lottery.

A Magdalen Dean of Divinity
Had a daughter who kept her virginity
The Fellows of Magdalen
Must have been dawdlin'
'Twould never have happened at Trinity.

Three men went to see a prostitute.

The first man came out from being with her and said, 'She's incredible. For five quid she'll do anything you want, as long as you tell her in three words.'

'What did you say?' asked the others.

'Shag me stupid,' he said, and walked off beaming.

The second man went in, and came out exhausted an hour later.

'Phew,' he said, 'she really will do anything.'

'What did you ask for,' said the last man.

'I said "lick me silly".' And he went off beaming.

The third man, who was Jewish, said to the woman, 'I hear that for five quid you will do anything, but I have to say what it is in three words.'

'Yes,' said the woman.

'Anything. In three words?'

'Yes,' smiled the woman seductively.

'OK, you're on,' he said. 'Paint my house.'

What's a DIY man's idea of contraception?
Cling-film condoms.